101 Things to Do the First Year of Your Divorce

Meg Connelly

Bloomington, IN Milton Keynes, UK

AuthorHouse™
1663 Liberty Drive, Suite 200
Bloomington, IN 47403
www.authorhouse.com
Phone: 1-800-839-8640

AuthorHouse™ UK Ltd.
500 Avebury Boulevard
Central Milton Keynes, MK9 2BE
www.authorhouse.co.uk
Phone: 08001974150

© 2006 Meg Connelly. All rights reserved.

*No part of this book may be reproduced, stored in
a retrieval system, or transmitted by any means
without the written permission of the author.*

First published by AuthorHouse 11/15/2006

ISBN: 978-1-4259-7688-0 (sc)

*Printed in the United States of America
Bloomington, Indiana*

This book is printed on acid-free paper.

Cover photo by Joe Crookes

This book is dedicated to my mother -
for letting me make my own mistakes and for
giving me the courage to admit when I had.

"What doesn't
kill me makes
me stronger."

-Albert Camus

Introduction

The first year of divorce has been described as the ultimate emotional rollercoaster ride. One can vacillate between intense sorrow and severe depression and unsurpassed exhilaration—freedom! For many new divorcees, the first year is made up of a combination of complex emotions, new responsibilities, and the anxiety that accompanies any new adventure. You've survived the divorce process, and now the avalanche of questions about your new life hit you with full force: What do I say? How do I act? Where do I go? Do I fit in? In short, WHAT DO I DO NOW? This book is intended to help you through that first year; to help you start over; to help you have fun. You get to begin again. Take advantage of it. Play with the "101 Things." Define yourself. Take a risk. Your new life gives you the opportunity not only to survive, but to thrive. You can! And you will!

Eighty percent of success is showing up.

Woody Allen (1935 -)

1. Accept all invitations.

Our lives improve only when we take chances - and the first and most difficult risk we can take is to be honest with ourselves.

Walter Anderson

2. Make a list of twenty things you like about yourself.

Frugality without creativity is deprivation.

Amy Dacyczyn

3. Peruse the "cheap-dates" section
   and take yourself out.

It's the friends you can call up at four a.m. that matter.

Marlene Dietrich (1901 - 1992)

4. Have lunch with a good listener
at the favorite restaurant of
you and your ex. Tell all the stories; joys and
tears.

Speak when you are angry—and you will make the best speech you'll ever regret.

Laurence J. Peter (1919 - 1988)

5. Try not to fight over money with your ex. If you must, avoid doing so verbally. E-mail; write letters; extinguish the conversation if it becomes inflammatory.

*Hope is the thing with
feathers
That perches in the soul.
And sings the tune
Without the words,
and never stops at all.*

Emily Dickinson (1830 - 1886)

6. Buy two Adirondack chairs.
(Let yourself hope.)

Not even the gods

fight against

necessity.

Simonides (556 BC - 468 BC)

7. Continue to drink coffee.

Respect a man, he will do the more.

James Howell

8. Insist on your own privacy and respect
that of your ex.
Never show up unannounced.
If the same consideration is not given to you,
keep your cool, rise above it, and do your
best to
model respectful behavior.

And the day came when the risk to remain tight in a bud was more painful than the risk it took to blossom.

Anais Nin (1903 - 1977)

9. Answer a personal ad.

All progress is based upon a universal innate desire on the part of every organism to live beyond its income.

Samuel Butler (1835 - 1902)

10. Do the remodel.

*Take rest;
a field that has
rested gives a
bountiful crop.*

Ovid (43 BC - 17 AD)

11. "Secure your mask before helping the person next to you."

(Take care of others,
but take care of yourself first.)

*It's not the voting
that's democracy,
it's the counting.*

Tom Stoppard (1937 -),
Jumpers (1972) act 1

12. Do the research, make your own
decision, and VOTE.

People often say that 'beauty is in the eye of the beholder,' and I say that the most liberating thing about beauty is realizing that you are the beholder. This empowers us to find beauty in places where others have not dared to look, including inside ourselves.

Salma Hayek

13. Buy beautiful, expensive lingerie and wear it.

*You may be deceived
if you trust too much,
but you will live in torment
if you do not trust enough.*

Frank Crane

14. Find a reliable, friendly handyman.
(And a mechanic!)

We make a living by what we get, we make a life by what we give.

Sir Winston Churchill (1874 - 1965)

15. Volunteer. Volunteer. Volunteer. The days of self-absorption (necessary for surviving a divorce) are over.

If a man does not make new acquaintances as he advances through life, he will soon find himself alone. A man should keep his friendships in constant repair.

Samuel Johnson (1709 - 1784)

16. Buy a stack of belated birthday cards
and send them to all the
folks you weren't thinking about the past few
years, because you were self-absorbed.

When they discover
the center of the
universe,
a lot of people
will be disappointed
to discover
they are not it.

Bernard Bailey

17. When a disgruntled child
calls from your ex's, listen,
but don't go save the day.

How poor are they who have not patience! What wound did ever heal but by degrees.

William Shakespeare (1564 - 1616)

18. Give yourself time before
you start dating. If you've
never been alone before, try it.
Give yourself three months,
give yourself six months;
whatever it takes for you to
learn that you can be alone
and be all right at the same time.

Truth is the only safe ground to stand on.

Elizabeth Cady Stanton (1815 - 1902)

19. Always tell the truth.
If you ever had a tantrum,
screamed like a banshee,
or threw something across the room, admit
it, own it, and then leave it behind.
Reinventing the past colors our future.
Building a new life requires carrying the
disappointment, the shame, and the sorrow
of a failed marriage.
This is enough to carry.
Why add the weight of fantasy or
disillusionment when the truth is almost
too much to bear as it is? People reinvent
the past so they can survive it. That's true.
But if the goal is thriving,
and not just surviving, then be honest
about the past so you can move on into the
future.

Health is not simply the absence of sickness.

Hannah Green

20. Masturbate.

Illusion is the first of all pleasures.

Oscar Wilde

21. Masturbate again.

Our envy of others

devours us

most of all.

Alexander Solzhenitsyn (1918 -)

22. Admire those happy, intact families that you see at the Fourth of July fireworks and accept your reaction to them.

Money frees you from doing things you dislike. Since I dislike doing nearly everything, money is handy.

Groucho Marx (1890 - 1977)

23. Meet with a financial planner.
Learn to live with less.

Never explain—your friends do not need it and your enemies will not believe you anyway.

Elbert Hubbard (1856 - 1915)

24. When people make jokes or disparaging comments about your ex, grin and bear it. They think they're helping. This is a time when "less is better." The less you say about your ex, the sooner the conversation will change to another topic. During the first year, you will find that people are curious about what happened. Some are considering divorce themselves. Others are seeking validation for their own choices. At times, you will want to share, and your experience will help others. Most of the time, a one-line response to inquiries about why you are divorced is adequate. "None of your @#%^ing business" may feel satisfying, but it's probably not the best choice. A brief statement that doesn't say much is best, for example, "It needed to happen"; or "Life can sure throw us some curve balls, can't it?"

Remember,
you are not obligated to explain
your circumstances to anybody!

If any one faculty of our nature may be called more wonderful than the rest, I do think it is memory. There seems something more speakingly incomprehensible in the powers, the failures, the inequalities of memory, than in any other of our intelligences. The memory is sometimes so retentive, so serviceable, so obedient; at others, so bewildered and so weak; and at others again, so tyrannic, so beyond control! We are, to be sure, a miracle every way; but our powers of recollecting and of forgetting do seem peculiarly past finding out.

Jane Austen (1775 - 1817), *Mansfield Park*

25. Give your photo album a makeover. Resist the urge to destroy the photos of your ex. "Bury" them for now. Who knows? There may be a day when they make you smile.

Like anyone else, there are days I feel beautiful and days I don't, and when I don't, I do something about it.

Cheryl Tiegs (1947 -), *O Magazine, May 2004*

26. Give yourself a makeover. Make the change you've always wanted to, but could never find the time nor the courage to.

I know nothing about sex because I was always married.

Zsa Zsa Gabor (1919 -)

27. Use condoms. An estimated one million people are currently living with HIV in the United States. There are forty thousand new infections occurring each year. Seventy percent of these new infections occur in men, and thirty percent occur in women. Seventy-five percent of the new infections in women are heterosexually transmitted. (http://www.until.org/statistics.shtml)

Grown-ups never understand anything for themselves, and it is tiresome for children to be always and forever explaining things to them.

Antoine de Saint-Exupery (1900 - 1944),
"The Little Prince", 1943

28. Your children are not messengers. Avoid
using them to carry information to your ex;
even insubstantial, trivial tidbits.
It is not their job. Take the responsibility
and be grateful for e-mail.

The worst loneliness is not to be comfortable with yourself.

Mark Twain (1835 - 1910)

29. Go to a movie by yourself. If it is your first time to go alone, try a matinee. You won't be the only one going solo.

To achieve the impossible dream, try going to sleep.

Joan Klempner

30. Buy a new mattress (out with the old) and put new, one hundred percent Egyptian, cotton sheets on it and sleep in the middle.

Treat the other man's faith gently; it is all he has to believe with. His mind was created for his own thoughts, not yours or mine.

Henry S. Haskins

31. Check out a variety of religious services.
Stay for the donuts.

Reality is that which, when you stop believing in it, doesn't go away.

Philip K. Dick (1928 - 1982)

32. Go to a wedding. Buy a new dress.
Sit in the back. Cry.

Life is a foreign language; all men mispronounce it.

Christopher Morley (1890 - 1957)

33. Stop comparing yourself to others.
We all move at our own pace, and life is
everything but a race.

An honor is not diminished for being shared.

Lois McMaster Bujold, *"Shards of Honor", 1986*

34. Stick to the custody agreement.
Down the road someday,
your children will thank you.
Children in times of upheaval
appreciate predictability.
If consistency is impossible, be flexible;
work toward it and celebrate small steps.

Forget injuries, never forget kindnesses.

Confucius (551 BC - 479 BC)

35. Don't be annoyed when people forget that you've gone back to using your maiden name. It's not important!

In silence man can most readily preserve his integrity.

Meister Eckhart

36. Never bash the opposite sex.
Avoid people who do.

There's only one way to have a happy marriage and as soon as I learn what it is I'll get married again.

Clint Eastwood (1930 -)

37. Be with people who love each other.
Watch and learn.

Creativity is a drug I cannot live without.

Cecil B. DeMille (1881 - 1959)

38. Paint your bedroom.
(Any color you want, baby.)

Risk! Risk anything! Care no more for the opinions of others, for those voices. Do the hardest thing on earth for you. Act for yourself. Face the truth.

Katherine Mansfield (1888 - 1923)

39. If you are feeling unappreciated and uninspired at work, say so. If things don't improve, quit. (Don't you sometimes wish that you had left your marriage earlier?)

Good manners will open doors that the best education cannot.

Clarence Thomas (1948 -)

40. Take your kids skiing or to a
fancy restaurant, whether or
not you can afford it.

Reminds me of my safari in Africa. Somebody forgot the corkscrew and for several days we had to live on nothing but food and water.

W. C. Fields (1880 - 1946)

41. Stop drinking.

I've never known any trouble that an hour's reading didn't assuage.

Charles De Secondat (1689 - 1755)

42. Get a new magazine subscription
and promise yourself that you'll
sit down and read it every month.

101 Things to Do the First Year of Your Divorce

If you cannot get rid of the family skeleton, you may as well make it dance.

George Bernard Shaw (1856 - 1950)

43. Dance.

The hatred you're carrying is a live coal in your heart – far more damaging to yourself than to them.

Lawana Blackwell,
The Dowry of Miss Lydia Clark, 1999

44. Never badmouth your spouse.
Figure out a way to unleash those negative
feelings in a way that truly unloads them.
Channel that energy into something creative
and positive. Complaining only seems to stir
things up. It doesn't accomplish anything.
Those feelings of hatred and resentment
will eventually seep away, but only if you let
them. Everyone has their own way of
getting past the negativity. Find yours.
Conversely, never praise your spouse.
Separated, neutral, and disinterested:
that is the goal.

Live well. It is the greatest revenge.

The Talmud

45. Stop dreaming about the slow,
painful death of your ex.
Now is the time for new dreams.

It is not a bad idea to get in the habit of writing down one's thoughts. It saves one having to bother anyone else with them.

Isabel Colegate

46. Write a goodbye "letter" to your ex.
This can be in any form –
perhaps a list of things you
no longer have to deal with,
or a collage of images.
Save it to peruse in a year or two.

Divorce is a game played by lawyers.

Cary Grant

47. Forgive yourself for paying your attorney
    too much. (Don't even total the bills!)

Happiness is having a large, loving, caring, close-knit family in another city.

George Burns (1896 - 1996)

48. Spend one-on-one time with your
parents and/or siblings.

Grief is the agony of an instant, the indulgence of grief the blunder of a life.

Benjamin Disraeli (1804 - 1881)

49. Stand in the shower and cry.

The greatest discovery of my generation is that a human being can alter his life by altering his attitudes of mind.

William James (1842 - 1910)

50. The only thing you can really control is
your attitude, so make a decision.
You can pick yourself up and live a life
filled with joy and peace.
All you have to do is decide to do it.

Anger makes you smaller, while forgiveness forces you to grow beyond what you were.

Cherie Carter-Scott, "
If Love Is a Game, These Are the Rules"

51. Let it go.

No one forgives with more grace and love than a child.

Real Live Preacher

52. Observe how readily children revert to peace after a quarrel. It really is what we all want. Make it happen.

In all things of nature there is something of the marvelous.

Aristotle (384 BC - 322 BC)

53. Watch a sunset.

Books are the quietest and most constant of friends; they are the most accessible and wisest of counsellors, and the most patient of teachers.

Charles W. Eliot (1834 - 1926)

54. Go to the library and take a book
off the shelf. Find a chair. Read.

The cure for boredom is curiosity. There is no cure for curiosity.

Dorothy Parker (1893 - 1967)

55. Go to an outdoor Shakespeare performance. They are often free!

Anger is a signal, and one worth listening to.

Harriet Lerner,
The Dance of Anger, 1985

56. Drive past your ex's house
and mutter obscenities
over and over again...

101 Things to Do the First Year of Your Divorce

Always forgive your enemies; nothing annoys them so much.

Oscar Wilde (1854 - 1900)

57. Drive past your ex's house and smile...
over and over again...

You can't separate peace from freedom because no one can be at peace unless he has his freedom.

Malcolm X (1925 - 1965)

58. Respect your ex's privacy.
Never show up unannounced.

Life engenders life. Energy creates energy. It is by spending oneself that one becomes rich.

Sarah Bernhardt (1844 - 1923)

59. Offer to help someone…and rejoice when that offer is accepted.

An excuse is worse than a lie, for an excuse is a lie, guarded.

Alexander Pope

60. Learn how to reject someone
without making excuses.

You have to stay in shape. My grandmother, she started walking five miles a day when she was 60. She's 97 today and we don't know where the hell she is.

Ellen Degeneres

61. Join a gym.

YMCAs are at the heart of community life across the country: 42 million families and 72 million households are located within three miles of a YMCA.

62. Check out the local YMCA.
These centers offer great opportunities
for single families.

First it is necessary to stand on your own two feet. But the minute a man finds himself in that position, the next thing he should do is reach out his arms.

Kristin Hunter,
O Magazine, November 2003

63. Throw a neighborhood party, and go
when the invitation is reciprocated.

If you can give your son or daughter only one gift, let it be enthusiasm.

Bruce Barton

64. Go camping with your kids
    and learn how to fish.

That's sort of a cliché about parents. We all believe that our children are the most beautiful children in the world. But the thing is, what no one really talks about is the fact that we all really believe it.

Heather Armstrong

65. Send a holiday card to your
ex-mother-in-law, but don't give her
your e-mail address.

Write something to suit yourself and many people will like it; write something to suit everybody and scarcely anyone will care for it.

Jesse Stuart

66. Write a letter to the editor.
Your voice is important!

Do not protect yourself by a fence, but rather by your friends.

Czech Proverb

67. Be a groupie. Find a musician,
a band, a writer, or an artist
and follow him or her.
Meet the other groupies.

Only I can change my life. No one can do it for me.

Carol Burnett (1936 -)

68. Take a risk.

I'll be floating like a butterfly and stinging like a bee.

Muhammad Ali

69. Give up control!
Float freely with the
newly discovered, almost
"unbearable lightness of being."

Irresponsibility is part of the pleasure of all art; it is the part the schools cannot recognize.

James Joyce

70. For one forty-eight hour period, absolutely refuse to get it together.

Politeness is half good manners and half good lying."

Mary Wilson Little

71. When people say, "I'm sorry about your divorce," resist the urge to say, "I'm not," and simply respond with, "Thank you."

Well, I know they've always told you/ Selfishness was wrong/ Yet it was for me, not you, I came to write this song/"

Neil Peart
(Canadian Drummer for
the band Rush b.1952)

72. Take a knitting class.
Make something for *yourself*.

*I like being single,
I'm always there
when I need me.*

Art Leo

73. Go to a singles event -
nothing ventured, nothing gained!

There are short-cuts to happiness, and dancing is one of them.

Vicki Baum

74. Learn to dance. Many cities have dance
    events every night of the week.

Bookcrossing.

the practice of leaving a book in a public place to be picked up and read by others, who then do likewise.

(added to the *Concise Oxford English Dictionary* in August 2004)
Check out http://www.bookcrossing.com/
The World's Biggest Book Club!!

75. Join a book club. Many bookstores host them monthly.

After an hour of "just a little more white, two squirts of blue, a dash of black, perhaps a tad more white," the paint-store clerk got my liter to the exact shade I wanted. With a sigh of relief, he pounded the lid on. "Now what do I do if I need more paint?" I asked. "Don't come back here," he begged.

76. Get a toolbox.
Amaze yourself (and your kids)
with all the repairs you can do yourself.

I'm living so far beyond my income that we may almost be said to be living apart.

e e cummings (1894 - 1962)

77. Decide on where you'd like to go
for a dream vacation and starting
saving for it now.

Manifest plainness,

Embrace simplicity,

Reduce selfishness,

Have few desires.

Lao-tzu (604 BC - 531 BC)

78. Go through your closets, drawers,
boxes, and bookcases and get rid of the
old stuff. You won't realize how heavy
it is until it's gone.

I have enough money to last me the rest of my life, unless I buy something.

Jackie Mason (1934 -)

79. Use only two credit cards.
Don't overspend. Buying things will
not erase the pain you feel. Being in
control of your life will.

You don't have to cook fancy or complicated masterpieces - just good food from fresh ingredients.

Julia Child (1912 -)

80. Buy an ethnic food cookbook and
    prepare something new.

The great art of giving consists in this: the gift should cost very little and yet be greatly coveted, so that it may be the more highly appreciated.

Baltasar Gracian

81. Donate or sell your wedding dress.
There are plenty of great marriages
out there. Be supportive!

The secret of staying young is to live honestly, eat slowly, and lie about your age.

Lucille Ball (1911 - 1989)

82. Don't avoid school reunions.
Remember, forty percent of marriages
end in divorce. You won't be the only one.
(http://www.divorcereform.org/rates.html)

"Pain is temporary. It may last a minute, or an hour, or a day, or a year, but eventually it will subside and something else will take its place. If I quit, however, it lasts forever."

Lance Armstrong

83. Go for a bike ride.
You were single once before,
and you can be single again.
It's just like riding a bike!

The brain is a wonderful organ. It starts working the moment you get up in the morning and does not stop until you get into the office.

Robert Frost (1874 - 1963)

84. Check out the experimental
college-class offerings at a local university.
They're inexpensive, geared toward adults,
and a great place to meet people who
share similar interests.

101 Things to Do the First Year of Your Divorce

I write entirely to find out what I'm thinking, what I'm looking at, what I see and what it means. What I want and what I fear.

Joan Didion (1934 -)

85. Keep a journal.

Grilling, broiling, barbecuing - whatever you want to call it - is an art, not just a matter of building a pyre and throwing on a piece of meat as a sacrifice to the gods of the STOMACH.

James Beard (1903-1985)

86. Learn how to barbeque.

If you have made mistakes, even serious ones, there is always another chance for you. What we call failure is not the falling down but the staying down.

Mary Pickford (1893 - 1979)

87. Forgive yourself.

Some are kissing mothers and some are scolding mothers, but it is love just the same.

Pearl Buck (1892 - 1973)

88. If you share custody of your children with your ex, try to live close to each other. Resist the urge to get as far away as possible, because your kids will forget things. You will be running back and forth. If the children can move easily between households, they will resent the new situation less. Do everything you can to make the new routine easier. Apologize to them and never, ever blame them for all the extra hassle.

Don't agonize.

Organize.

Florence Kennedy

89. Enjoy having your living space to yourself. Your closet just doubled in size! Organize it!

Ask about your neighbors, then buy the house.

Jewish Proverb

90. Get to know your neighbors.
Set up an emergency plan with them.

"Americans, who make more of marrying for love than any other people, also break up more of their marriages, but the figure reflects not so much the failure of love as the determination of people not to live without it."

Morton Hunt

91. Try online dating. Be safe and don't expect too much. At the very least, you'll meet someone for coffee and have a pleasant conversation.
(You'll be amazed at how many single people are out there.)

The art of mothering is to teach the art of living to children.

Elain Heffner,
O Magazine, May 2003

92. Always put the kids first.
And remember, sometimes what's best
for the kids is Mom or Dad getting out
and doing what she or he wants to do!

In the absence of clearly-defined goals, we become strangely loyal to performing daily trivia until ultimately we become enslaved by it.

Robert Heinlein (1907 - 1988)

93. Write a description of the person you want to be. It can be any kind of description you want: an essay, a list, a visual, or just a few adjectives. Make a plan of how you can become that person. Think of small things you can do each day to reach your goal.

101 Things to Do the First Year of Your Divorce

"I've never tried to block out the memories of the past, even though some are painful. I don't understand people who hide from their past. Everything you live through helps to make you the person you are now."

Sophia Loren (1934 -   )

94. Find a beautiful box for keepsakes
from your old life.

Before God we are all equally wise – and equally foolish.

Albert Einstein (1879 - 1955)

95. Try to realize that all people make
assumptions. Some people will make
assumptions about your situation.
If it bothers you, explain your situation
and clear things up. When you are sad
and feeling lonely, it's easy to assume
that everyone around you is happy. Don't
assume that, because it probably isn't true.
Everybody has their share of grief; some
more than others. You just happen to be
experiencing a bit of yours right now.

101 Things to Do the First Year of Your Divorce

I have only one superstition. I touch all the bases when I hit a home run.

Babe Ruth (1895 - 1948)

96. Allow yourself silly rituals
such as collecting tokens
or making wishes.
Why not?

Time is the coin of your life. It is the only coin you have, and only you can determine how it will be spent. Be careful lest you let other people spend it for you.

Carl Sandburg (1878 - 1967)

97. Don't be a "Divorce Magnet."
This happens when friends and
acquaintances dump their marital woes
on you expecting an empathetic ear.
Don't let it happen. Change the subject.
If all else fails, suggest counseling and
run away! Your time and energy is very
valuable this year. Use it for yourself and
your family. It's not being selfish.
It's being realistic.

We must be willing to get rid of the life we've planned, so as to have the life that is waiting for us.

Joseph Campbell (1904 - 1987)

98. Take baby steps.
Rome wasn't built in a day.

He not busy being born is busy dying.

Bob Dylan (1941 -)

99. Rewrite your will.

*Life shrinks
or expands in
proportion
to one's courage.*

Anais Nin (1903 – 1977)

100. Write a self-help book.

"Reaching that windswept perch, I decided, would cleanse my spirit and heal my wounds. More than that, it would send me home with a title: The First American Woman to Climb Everest."

Stacy Allison

101. Divorce is a beginning.
It's the beginning of a climb.
It's the beginning of a climb
to a new life; to a new you.

There will be peaks and valleys along
the way and it will take a long time,
but you can make it to the top.
So decide which mountain you want to
conquer. Then take the first step.

Acknowledgements

I'd like to thank my family, friends and coworkers who supported me through my first year of divorce. I'd also like to thank the other divorcees who shared their stories with me. From these tales of joy and woe I found laughter, encouragement, and insight. I incorporated what I learned from them in this book so others could find hope as well.

Thank-you!!

Made in the USA
Lexington, KY
22 July 2010